ELLEN MACARTHUR

UNAUTHORISED BIOGRAPHY

Claire Throp

www.raintreepublishers.co.uk
Visit our website to find out more information about Raintree books.

To order:
☎ Phone +44 (0) 1865 888066
🖷 Fax +44 (0) 1865 314091
💻 Visit www.raintreepublishers.co.uk

Editorial: Catherine Veitch
Design: Richard Parker and Q2A Solutions
Illustrations: Oxford Designers and Illustrators
Picture research: Mica Brancic

Originated by DOT Gradations Ltd
Printed and bound in China by CTPS

ISBN 978 1 4062 0956 3 (hardback)
12 11 10 09 08
10 9 8 7 6 5 4 3 2 1

ISBN 978 1 4062 0964 8 (paperback)
14 13 12 11 10
10 9 8 7 6 5 4 3 2 1

British Library Cataloguing in Publication Data
Throp, Claire
Ellen MacArthur.—(Sport files)
797.1'24'092
A full catalogue record for this book is available from the British Library.

Acknowledgements
The publishers would like to thank the following for permission to reproduce photographs:
© Action Images pp. **6** and **9** (DPPI), **7** and **12** (Jacques Vapillion/DPPI), **8** (ellenmacarthur.com/DPPI), **22** (DPPI/Vincent Curutchet); © PA Archive/ PA Photos pp. **18**, **21**, **26** and **27** (Chris Ison); © Reuters pp. **5** (Stephen Hird), **15** (Action Images), **17** (John Downing), **19** (Charles Platiau/Action Images), **25** (Kirsty Wigglesworth/Action Images).

Cover photograph of English skipper Ellen MacArthur posing on the docks of Saint-Malo harbour, reproduced with permission of ©Getty Images/AFP/Martin Bureau.

Every effort has been made to contact copyright holders of material reproduced in this book. Any omissions will be rectified in subsequent printings if notice is given to the publishers.

CONTENTS

Some words are shown in bold, **like this**. You can find out what they mean by looking in the glossary.

Ellen MacArthur is one of the world's greatest sailors who has created many world records. She held the fastest **solo** time for travelling around the world (in 2004–5) – until this time was beaten by Francis Joyon in January 2008. During her round-the-world trip Ellen also broke many other sailing records. What makes this even more special is that she is a woman, only 1.60 m (5 ft 3 in) in height, who at the start of her career was not rich. Ellen has used strength, determination, and will-power to reach her goals.

Ellen was just 24 years old when she first came into the public eye. She came second in the **Vendée Globe**, one of the most difficult races that a sailor can compete in. She was the youngest to complete the race and the fastest woman to sail around the world. In this race Ellen proved that women can compete with 'rich men' in sailing.

FAST FACT FILE

Name:	Ellen MacArthur
Born:	8 July 1976, near Whatstandwell, Derbyshire
Height:	1.60 m (5 ft 3 in)
Family:	Mum Avril, dad Ken, brothers Lewis and Fergus
First boat:	*Threep'ny Bit*
Records:	
2000-01:	Fastest woman to complete the Vendée Globe
2002:	New **monohull** record in Route du Rhum
2004-05:	Fastest solo round-the-world voyage
Honours:	
1995:	Young Sailor of the Year
1999:	YJA/BT Yachtsman of the Year
2001:	**MBE**
2005:	Dame Commander of the Order of the British Empire
Charity:	The Ellen MacArthur Trust

Ellen MacArthur arrives back in Falmouth, Cornwall in February 2005 after her solo record trip around the world.

Ellen holds several speed records that are approved by the World Sailing Speed Racing Council (WSSRC). She has sailed over 250,000 **nautical miles** or about 11 times around the world.

Ellen has won many awards. She was voted *Sunday Times* Sportswoman of the Year in 2001, she has been runner up in the BBC Sports Personality of the Year twice, and in 2005 she was honoured by the queen. She is now known as **Dame** Ellen MacArthur.

Ellen MacArthur was born on 8 July 1976 near Whatstandwell in Derbyshire. Ellen's parents, Avril and Ken, were both teachers. Ellen had an elder brother, Lewis, and a younger brother, Fergus.

Ellen was a tomboy. She liked having adventures in the fields around the family home, reading books about spies, and playing games of cricket with her grandpa. Her family lived on a smallholding, which is a small farm. This meant there was plenty of wide open space to play in.

A trip on *Cabaret*

Ellen first became interested in the sea when she was just four years old. That year she was told she was too young to join her brother Lewis on a trip on their Auntie Thea's boat, *Cabaret*. However, the following year she was allowed to go with them. Ellen loved the experience and wanted to know everything that her aunt could tell her about sailing.

Ellen loves all boats. Here Ellen, aged six, joins her grandfather on board a submarine.

Ellen and her family are close, and they supported her in her struggles to succeed in sailing.

When Ellen got home from this trip she started to save money to put towards buying a boat of her own. She even saved part of her school dinner money each day. She read sailing books and magazines and sent off for leaflets with pictures of boats in.

Ellen got a chance to sail on her own for the first time in the French **port** of Dunkirk. She sailed in a sailing **dinghy** bought by her aunt to pull along behind *Cabaret*. A dinghy is a small open boat, with a mast and sails. It gave Ellen a sense of freedom and love for the sea.

Now Ellen wanted to buy her own boat more than ever. When she found the boat she wanted she had only saved £200. The boat cost £535. Ellen's nan knew how much she wanted the boat so decided to give Ellen and her brothers a treat – £300 each! Finally, Ellen was able to buy her first boat. She called it *Threep'ny Bit*.

For her tenth birthday, Ellen went on a week-long race training camp at Rutland Water. She was one of the youngest to take part. She **capsized** eleven times on the first day, but she learned a lot. At the end of the week she was determined never to come last in a race again.

Animal lover

Ellen was 13 when she heard about some puppies that would have to be put down if homes were not found for them. She talked to her mum and dad and was finally allowed to keep Mac, a Border Collie cross. The next year, because of her love of animals, Ellen did some work experience at a veterinary surgery. She then decided that she wanted to become a vet.

A couple of years later, Ellen bought another boat, which she called *Kestrel*. As soon as Ellen finished her GCSEs, she started to learn as much as she could about boat-building. She spent two summers working on *Kestrel*, turning her into a boat she could be proud of.

When her parents saw how **committed** Ellen was to *Kestrel*, they decided that she should learn how to sail properly. When she was 16 Ellen went on a sailing course at David King Nautical School in Hull.

Walks with Mac were a good way to take a break from working on Kestrel.

Ellen loved going out on Iduna.

Illness hits

In the first year of her A-levels, Ellen caught glandular fever, which is an illness that makes parts of the neck become swollen and can make you feel very tired. While she was getting better, Ellen watched the Whitbread round-the-world race on television. After watching the race she decided to buy another boat. This one was 6 metres (21 feet) long. She called it *Iduna*.

A change of mind

After her illness, Ellen gave up on the idea of becoming a vet. It was very hard to get onto veterinary courses at university and Ellen had missed a lot of school through illness. She decided that sailing was now her number one interest. She was going to become a sailor.

After a while, Ellen was allowed to start teaching at David King's Nautical School. She was only 17 and was now standing in front of adults teaching them how to sail! Ellen taught during the day and worked on making *Iduna* **seaworthy** at night.

The first big challenge that she set herself was to sail around Britain **solo**. This meant that she would be sailing the boat on her own. It was 1995 and Ellen was 18 – she was very excited about the idea but needed some money for the journey. A company called Musto, which made sailing gear, agreed to **sponsor** Ellen. She then had to plan her trip. She had to find out the distance between **ports**, and plan the best route between them. She had to take into account what the winds and weather might be like at that time of year, and even whether food would be available. Ellen also had to make sure that *Iduna* had been tested in sea conditions similar to those that she would meet on her journey.

Ellen was finally ready to leave on 1 June 1995. Her family waved goodbye as she set off from Hull. When Ellen reached Hartlepool storms and huge waves meant she got stuck there for two weeks. Then when she reached Montrose in Scotland, she had terrible stomach cramps for several days. Further up the Scottish coast, Ellen had a nicer experience: she was accompanied by wild dolphins, which swam alongside the boat.

SPONSORSHIP

Many sports, particularly sailing, require a lot of money. Sponsorship can be vital. Companies agree to give money and in return the sportsperson or team must display the company's **logo**. For example, boats are often named after their sponsors.

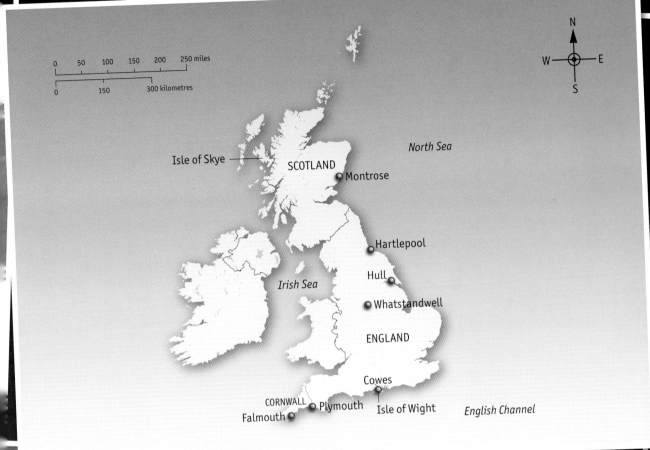

This map shows some of the places Ellen visited on her sail around Britain.

On 12 October Ellen sailed back into Hull. As well as her family and friends, there were also journalists and photographers waiting to welcome her. It had been a big challenge for Ellen, but she had coped with it well. As she said herself: "I grew up on that trip around Britain."

Tough times followed the round-Britain trip as Ellen had to deal with various family difficulties, including her dad falling off a ladder and badly damaging his back.

Ellen did, however, meet her future business partner, Mark Turner. He had heard about her trip and encouraged her to compete in the **Mini Transat**. At that time the Mini Transat race took place every two years, with boats setting off from France and finishing in Martinique. (From 2009 it will end in Brazil and take place every four years.) It is a difficult, and very dangerous race, that has claimed several lives. Ellen knew she'd have to be fully prepared.

Ellen had no money at the time and was living in a temporary home. She wrote over 2,000 letters to companies looking for **sponsorship** and received only two replies. In the end she tried to get money in France, where sailing is far more popular than in Britain. She managed to get enough money together to buy a boat called *Le Poisson*. Ellen then rebuilt the boat herself, which meant that she had to learn French quickly!

Ellen was one of only two English competitors in the Mini Transat. The other was her business partner, Mark. She was also the only woman in the race.

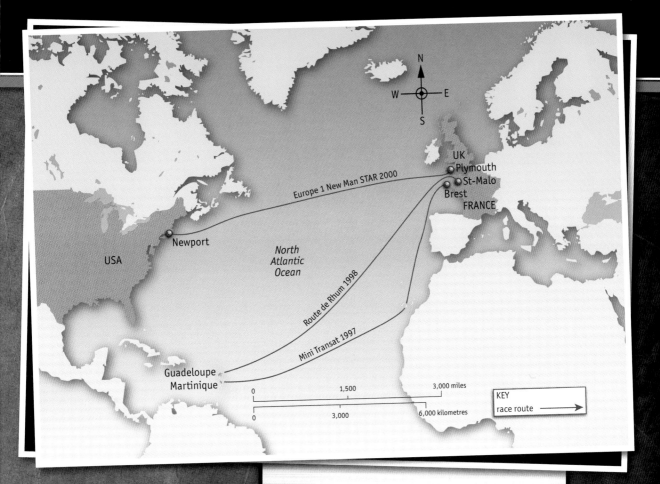

This map shows the transatlantic (across the Atlantic Ocean) race routes.

In 1997 Ellen took part in the Mini Transat – her first **solo** race. The race took 33 days, and she finished 17th. This result brought sponsorship from Kingfisher, a group that owned various shops in the UK.

In 1998 Ellen received some sad news. Her nan, who had been ill for some time, died of the disease cancer. Ellen was very upset at her death.

After the Mini Transat race, Ellen had no money. She wanted to enter the Route du Rhum, but couldn't afford it. She discovered at the last minute that her nan had left her some money. More money was gathered together and she entered the race. She ended up winning her class and finishing fifth overall. In January 1999 she was named BT/YJA Yachtsman of the Year.

In February 2000 *Kingfisher* was **launched** in New Zealand. The boat had been designed by four people and had taken five months to build. It was named after Ellen's **sponsor** Kingfisher. On the water Ellen and the team tested the boat and finally it was ready. Ellen was able to sail back to Europe from New Zealand, which gave her experience of how to handle the boat on the open sea. This was good preparation for the challenges ahead.

It wasn't all good

While Ellen was extremely excited about the launch of *Kingfisher*, it happened at the same time as she split up from her boyfriend, Merv. He had been part of the team that had designed and built *Kingfisher* and the stress of all the work put too much of a strain on their relationship.

TEAMWORK

Although Ellen races in the boats alone, she does not work alone. There are other people working behind the scenes to make sure the boats can cope with record attempts and race situations. There are people who design the boats, those who make them, and others who test the boats for safety. There are also people who work out the sponsorship deals. Ellen herself has said this about the people she works with: "Those people are as much a part of the team as you are. It just happens that you are the person that has to go in front of the camera."

Racing in her newly built boat, Kingfisher, *Ellen won the Europe 1 New Man STAR.*

Later in the year, Ellen raced *Kingfisher* for the first time in the Europe 1 New Man STAR **solo transatlantic** race, which started in Plymouth and finished in Newport, USA (see map on page 13). She was nervous because she didn't know how well the boat was going to race. In the end, Ellen had no need to worry: she won the Open 60 class. This was despite sleeping for only about four hours on each of the race's fourteen days. She was the youngest person ever to win the race.

Ellen was exhausted after winning the race. She was able to go home and see her family, but also had to do a number of interviews about her victory. Finally, Ellen was able to get away for a break. She went to the Alps, where she spent a couple of days climbing in the mountains.

In November 2000, Ellen and 23 other sailors were ready at Les Sables d'Olonne, France, for the start of the **Vendée Globe solo**, non-stop, round-the-world race (see map on page 23). A storm meant that the race was delayed for two days. Finally, after sad goodbyes to her parents and her boyfriend, Ian, the race began.

Ellen had to repair her boat many times and even had to climb the mast twice in one day. In the Southern Ocean she woke up one morning to find that the boat had just missed a 12 metre (40 foot) iceberg.

By the end of December, after nearly two months at sea, Ellen was exhausted. News that some sailors had claimed she had cheated on the Europe 1 STAR race pushed her on: "It was the biggest kick-start I could have had." About a week after this Ellen was in second place in the race.

On 29 January Ellen was in the lead for a short time. Shortly afterwards, the boat hit something and was badly damaged. Ellen was now in second place again. The mast was then damaged, which meant *Kingfisher* was unable to sail at full speed again. Ellen could no longer win the race. She was still the fastest woman and youngest sailor to ever complete the race when she crossed the line on 11 February 2001.

FINAL POSITIONS OF THE VENDÉE GLOBE

Position	Names	Country	Name of boat	Time
1	Michel Desjoyeaux	France	*PRB*	93 days 3 hours 57 minutes
2	Ellen MacArthur	Great Britain	*Kingfisher*	94 days 4 hours 25 minutes
3	Roland Jourdain	France	*Sill Matines La Potagere*	96 days 1 hour 2 minutes

Ellen had to make several dangerous climbs up Kingfisher's *mast during the race, in order to make repairs.*

She's a winner!

The sailing world had finally started to take notice of Ellen. She won the FICO Lacoste Offshore World Championship. Ellen was also given many awards and honours. She received an **MBE** and won the Helen Rollason award for courage and achievement in the face of **adversity**. She was also runner up in the BBC Sports Personality of the Year award. Ellen was now a well-known sports star.

As Ellen herself said: "When I finished the **Vendée Globe** in 2001 I was 24 years old and suddenly went from being nobody to being somebody who people knew. That's quite a big change." Coping with that change was yet another thing that Ellen had to work hard at. One of the things that helped her get through that period was a family holiday on the Isle of Skye, Scotland (see map on page 11). While there she started looking into her family's history. Her parents both came from Scotland and she found out that her dad's family were fishermen who lived on the Isle of Skye. She was thrilled to find a connection to the sea in her family.

An emotional day

Ellen had been given several awards and prizes after her Vendée triumph. At the beginning of 2002, she was given another: an **honorary degree** from the University of Derby. It was an award to recognise her achievements in sailing and her work for children's charities. This was the university where her nan had got her degree while battling cancer. It was an emotional day for Ellen and she broke down in tears before she could finish her speech.

Ellen received an honorary degree from the University of Derby.

The Route du Rhum race covered St Malo, France to Pointe-a-Pitre, Guadeloupe (see map on page 13).

Also in January, Ellen and her sponsors Kingfisher announced a five-year plan. One of the things that Ellen said she wanted to do was make an attempt at the **Jules Verne record**. This was the record for the fastest round-the-world trip in a **crewed** boat.

The Route du Rhum 2002

In the meantime, Ellen's next challenge, the Route du Rhum race began on 9 November 2002. Ellen was racing *Kingfisher* for the last time. There were various problems with the boat, including nearly losing the **mast** and catching something in the **rudder** under the boat. But on 23 November, Ellen came home first in the **monohull** class. She had set a new record for the class.

CHARITY WORK

Ellen worked with French charity A Chacun son Cap (French for "Everyone has a goal") during the summer of 2000. The charity took children who had the disease leukaemia, or were recovering from it, sailing. The trips brought the children together and allowed them to talk to each other about their illness and recovery. Ellen was so moved by the trip that she decided to set up a similar charity in the UK.

In January 2003 she began The Ellen MacArthur Trust. The Trust takes groups of children sailing for four days. They set off from Cowes on the Isle of Wight (see map on page 11) on 11.5–13.7 metre (38–45 foot) cruising yachts. The children live on board and the yachts stop in a different **port** every night. It allows the children to enjoy something they wouldn't normally get to do. The experience is an adventure and also helps them to think about something other than their illness for a short time.

Other sailors such as Shirley Robertson also work with Ellen for the charity. Shirley won gold medals for sailing in the 2000 and 2004 Olympics. Either Ellen or Shirley, or sometimes both, try to join the children for a day on each of the trips that take place.

FAILED ATTEMPTS

Along with her **crew** of 14, Ellen attempted to break the **Jules Verne record** in 2003. This record is for the fastest route possible around the world. The attempt failed because of a broken **mast** on her boat *Kingfisher II*. Ellen was obviously disappointed but was very proud of her crew. Everyone had tried their best.

The Ellen MacArthur Trust helps many children to begin enjoying their lives again after serious illness. Here, Ellen joins a group of children who have had cancer. They are going to sail on the boat Scarlet Oyster, at Cowes, Isle of Wight.

Ellen had been sailing in **multihulls** since 2001. Multihulls are boats with two or more hulls joined together. In June 2004 she made a **solo transatlantic** record attempt on board a new boat *B&Q*. *B&Q* was a **trimaran launched** in January 2004. This record attempt involved sailing from New York, USA to Cornwall, UK. Sadly, she missed the record by just 75 minutes.

From November 2004 to February 2005, Ellen attempted to break yet another record. This time it was the round-the-world record in *B&Q*. Ellen had 12 cameras on board and kept **video diaries** of the journey. She sailed 44,022 kilometres (27,354 miles). Many records were picked up along the way, including the fastest **solo equator**-to-equator time.

It wasn't easy...

As always the trip wasn't easy. Only two weeks into the journey the **generator** broke down and Ellen badly burnt her arm trying to repair it. She then had to cope with storms in the Southern Ocean. There were also icebergs, very strong winds, and 15 metre (50 foot) waves. At one point she had five days without wind, which slowed her down. Ellen even had to avoid a meeting with a whale, which nearly swam into her boat.

The worst problem was when one of the sails broke away from the top of the **mast**. This had to be repaired by Ellen, or the record attempt would be over. She had to climb the mast to fix it and got very bashed and bruised. She said in a video diary: "I'm pretty sore really. Every time I try and sleep, I wake up sweating and feeling like I've been in a fight."

Ellen made the trip around the world in just 71 days, 14 hours, 18 minutes, and 33 seconds.

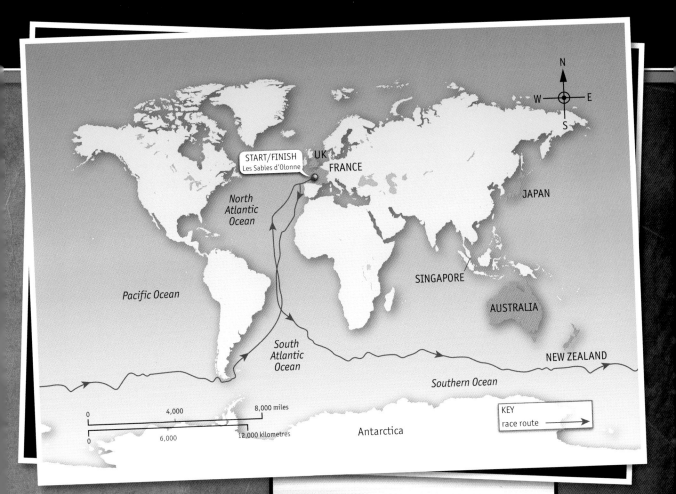

This map shows the route taken by Ellen on her round-the-world trips.

She made it!

It had been a major achievement in 2004 by Frenchman Francis Joyon to set the record. Not many people thought that Ellen would be able to beat his record, and certainly not on her first attempt. Even Ellen herself had had doubts. However, she made it and broke the record by more than a day.

In January 2008, Joyon broke Ellen's record by more than 14 days. She was there in France to congratulate him but was keen to point out that "records are made to be broken". Perhaps Ellen will have another go at the record at some point in the future?

Thousands of people had gathered at Falmouth in Cornwall to greet Ellen at the end of her round-the-world record attempt. Messages of congratulations came from many different people including the prime minister at the time, Tony Blair, and the Queen. But again Ellen wanted to praise the people behind the scenes: "The best feeling I had in the whole around-the-world record was the feeling of team work. And that's bizarre to think that you've raced around the world to break a record on your own but actually the biggest thing was the team."

When Ellen was made a Dame, it is thought she was the youngest person to receive this highest royal honour. She was also awarded the honorary naval rank of Lieutenant Commander in the Royal Navy Reserve. Then at the end of 2005, she was voted runner up in the BBC Sports Personality of Year. This time she came second to cricketer, Andrew Flintoff.

Sailing with a crew

In 2006 Ellen got back to sailing with a **crew**. The Asian Record Circuit allowed Ellen's team to set new world records for each part of a journey that included nine **ports**. The circuit started in Japan and ended in Singapore. Other teams will now be able to challenge themselves in breaking the records in the future.

THE HONOURS SYSTEM

Honours are awards given for exceptional achievement, service, or bravery. Anyone can recommend a person for an honour. Decisions are made by the prime minister and his or her ministers and passed on to the Queen. A person can be made an **MBE** (as Ellen was in 2001), an OBE, a Dame (women only) or Knight (men only). A woman who has been made a Dame can then add "Dame" in front of her name. A ceremony, called an investiture, follows and here the Queen presents the person with their badge, medal, or ribbon, which represents the Honour.

At times Ellen has received criticism about not wanting to sail with crews. But she points out that that is not the case: "It's a fantastic experience sailing with a crew and something I've done a lot of on *B&Q*, although people are generally not aware of that."

Dame Ellen holds up her medal on the day she met the Queen.

In September 2007 a three-year **sponsorship** deal between Ellen's team and British Telecom (BT) was announced. It will allow the team to get involved in more races and events. In return Ellen has become an **ambassador** for BT's Better world programme. It focuses on acting responsibly towards the environment, for example by encouraging people to not waste energy.

Ellen also hopes to use her fame to make people more aware of other environmental issues, such as the need to protect the albatross (seabird) in Antarctica. At a special event in October 2007, set up by **WWF**, the wildlife protection group, Ellen gave a talk on her experiences in South Georgia and on the Southern Ocean.

Criticism

Some people have criticised Ellen and tried to put her success down to technology. They say that her achievements cannot be compared to previous records because the boats she has sailed on are far more advanced technologically than for example Sir Robin Knox Johnston's was when he broke the round-the-world record in 1968–69. However, this could probably be said about other sports too.

Ellen attended a press conference in Barcelona to launch a new race, the Barcelona World Race.

Ellen has worked extremely hard to get where she has. Her talent has allowed her to become one of the best known sailors in Britain.

People have also made fun of Ellen for making a **video diary** on all her journeys. However, she has argued: "I have always wanted to share as much of my experiences as I possibly can ... if you don't capture it, it's gone forever."

Ellen now lives in Cowes on the Isle of Wight. Offshore Challenges is also based there. She loves spending time in Cowes whenever she can – visiting boatyards or going for runs along the beach.

Role model

Ellen has been a great example of the fact that women have a place in sport. She has proved with all her success that sailing is not just for men. Her hard work and dedication to the sport have meant that she is a **role model** for girls. She has also shown that it is not necessary to have lots of money to compete. If someone really wants something they can achieve it.

8 July 1976	Ellen MacArthur is born in Whatstandwell, Derbyshire.
1981	Ellen has her first sailing trip on Auntie Thea's boat, *Cabaret*.
1985	Ellen buys her first boat, an 8-foot **dinghy**, called *Threep'ny Bit*.
1994	Ellen teaches sailing to adults at the David King Nautical School in Hull.
June–October 1995	Ellen sails single-handedly around Britain in *Iduna*.
1995	Ellen receives the BT/YJA Young Sailor of Year award.
1997	Ellen sails *Le Poisson* in the **Mini Transat solo** race, finishing 17th.
1998	Ellen secures **sponsorship** from Kingfisher.
November 1998	Ellen wins her class in the Route du Rhum and comes fifth overall.
1999	Ellen wins BT/YJA Yachtsman of the Year.
June 2000	Ellen wins her class in the Europe 1 New Man STAR **transatlantic** race.
February 2001	Ellen comes second in the **Vendée Globe** solo round-the-world race.
2001	Ellen is awarded an **MBE**.
January 2002	Ellen receives an **honary degree** from the University of Derby.
9–23 November 2002	Ellen wins the Route du Rhum.
February 2003	Ellen captains a failed round-the-world record attempt for a **crewed** yacht.
June 2004	Ellen fails in her attempt to break the west–east transatlantic crossing record.
28 Nov 2004–7 Feb 2005	Ellen breaks the solo record for sailing non-stop around the world.
February 2005	Ellen is made a **Dame** Commander of the Order of the British Empire.
September 2007	Ellen announces a three-year sponsorship deal with BT.
January 2008	Francis Joyon broke Ellen's 2004–5 record for **solo** round-the-world trip.

Amazing facts

▲ Ellen was given the official title "Sailing's Young Hope" by the French after her performance in the 2001 Vendée Globe.

▲ Ellen had the fastest time in the television programme *Top Gear*'s Star in a reasonably-priced car challenge until the 8th series. She drove one lap of a racetrack in 1 minute 46.7 seconds!

▲ Ellen passed her driving test on the second attempt.

▲ On board the boat, Ellen has to eat freeze-dried food because it has to keep for long periods of time while she's out on the sea. She also has to take extra vitamins to keep her healthy.

▲ During the Vendée Globe race, Ellen celebrated Christmas. She even had a mini Christmas tree with tinsel!

▲ Ellen can communicate with people on dry land via a satellite phone on board.

▲ Ellen can speak French fluently.

▲ Ellen has an asteroid named after her – 20043 Ellenmacarthur.

▲ When Ellen was saving up for her second boat, *Kestrel* she drew a graph with 100 squares on it. Every time she managed to save £1 she ticked a box.

GLOSSARY

adversity hardship, difficulties

ambassador person who represents a group of people or project

capsize overturn

commit be willing to put in a lot of time and effort on a particular project

crew group of people who work on a boat or ship

Dame title given to a woman who has been honoured by the Queen

dinghy small, open boat, with a mast and sails

equator imaginary circle around the Earth

generator machine that creates electrical energy

honorary degree degree that is presented to someone by a university for something they have done in their public life, rather than a qualification achieved through the taking of exams

Jules Verne record challenge for fully-crewed boats to achieve the fastest sailing time around the world

launch in sailing, when a boat sets off on its first journey

logo symbol used for easy recognition of a company

mast tall, vertical pole on a boat to which the sails are connected

MBE Member of the British Empire. It is given to a person in recognition for something that they have achieved.

Mini Transat race that previously took place every two years, beginning in France and finishing in Martinique. From 2009 it will be held every four years, and end in Salvador da Bahia, in Brazil.

monohull boat with only one hull

multihull boat with more than one hull. The hull is the main body of the boat.

nautical mile unit of measurement for sea navigation. At 1,853 kilometres (1,151 miles), it is just over a mile long.

port harbour

role model person who is a good example to others

rudder vertical fin at the stern (rear of the boat) that is used to steer the boat

seaworthy boat or ship that is ready to sail on the sea

solo alone

sponsor give money in order to fund a project or team

transatlantic to or from the other side of the Atlantic Ocean

trimaran three-hulled boat

Vendée Globe solo, non-stop race round-the-world that takes place every four years

video diary filmed daily record of events and experiences

WWF World Wildlife Fund. WWF is an organization that works to protect animals around the world.

Useful address

Royal Yachting Association
RYA House
Ensign Way
Hamble, Southampton Hampshire,
SO31 4YA

http://www.rya.org.uk/
The RYA's website should help you find a sailing club or training group to join near your area.

Books

Livewire Real Lives: *Ellen MacArthur*, Mike Wilson (Hodder Arnold, 2006)

RYA Go Sailing: *A Practical Guide for Young People*, Claudia Myatt
        (Royal Yachting Association, 2005)

Solo Sailing, Esther Ripley (Dorling Kindersley, 2005)

Websites

http://www.ellenmacarthur.com/
This is Ellen's own website. It gives information about her past successes, as well as news about her future plans.

http://www.ellenmacarthurtrust.org
This site looks at Ellen's charity and what it does.

http://www.btteamellen.com/
Team Ellen is a partnership with British Telecom that will help Ellen to be successful in new challenges over the next three years.

Disclaimer

All the Internet addresses (URLs) given in this book were valid at the time of going to press. However, due to the dynamic nature of the Internet, some addresses may have changed, or sites may have changed or ceased to exist since publication. While the author and Publishers regret any inconvenience this may cause readers, no responsibility for any such changes can be accepted by either the author or the Publishers. It is recommended that adults supervise children on the Internet.